Oceans

By John Wood

BookLife

©2018
Book Life
King's Lynn
Norfolk PE30 4LS

ISBN: 978-1-78637-133-1

Written by:
John Wood

Edited by:
Holly Duhig

Designed by:
Matt Rumbelow

A catalogue record for this book
is available from the British Library.

CONTENTS

Words that look like this can be found in the glossary on page 24.

WHAT IS A HABITAT?

A habitat is a place where an animal lives. It provides the animal with food, shelter and everything else it needs to survive.

There are lots of different habitats in the world. Each one is home to many different animals.

Rainforests

The Arctic

Forests

Mountains

Deserts

WHAT ARE

OCEANS?

Oceans are large areas of water between continents. Ocean water is called saltwater, because it contains a lot of salt.

Almost three quarters of the Earth's surface is covered by oceans.

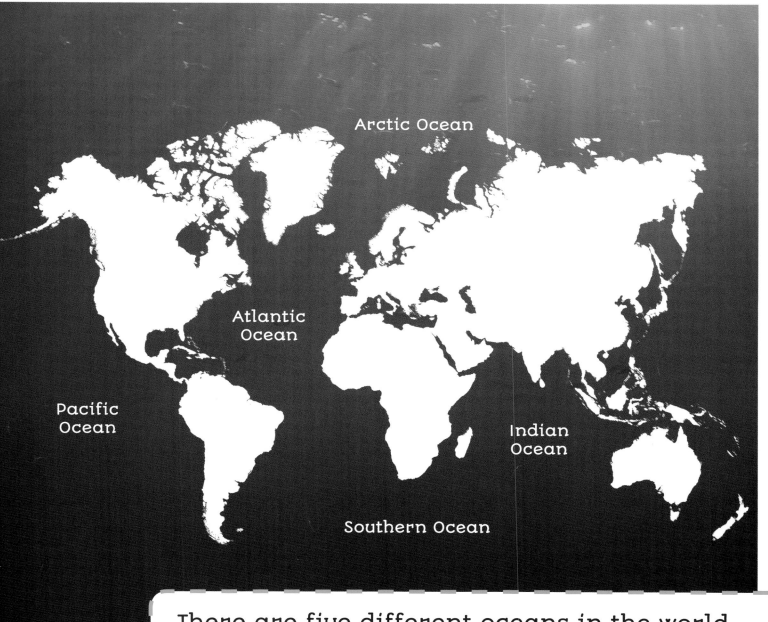

Arctic Ocean

Atlantic
Ocean

Pacific
Ocean

Indian
Ocean

Southern Ocean

There are five different oceans in the world.
Their names are the Arctic, Atlantic, Indian,
Pacific and Southern oceans. Together they
are called the World Ocean.

TYPES OF
OCEAN HABITAT

There are many habitats in the ocean. Big animals often live in the open ocean. Smaller animals often live in shallow waters. Some animals live in ocean trenches.

Corals are living things that are hard and stony. Lots of corals together make a coral reef. Lots of creatures make their homes here.

The Great Barrier Reef, Australia

CLOWNFISH

Clownfish make their homes among the tentacles of an anemone. An anemone lives in a coral reef and stings most animals, but not the clownfish.

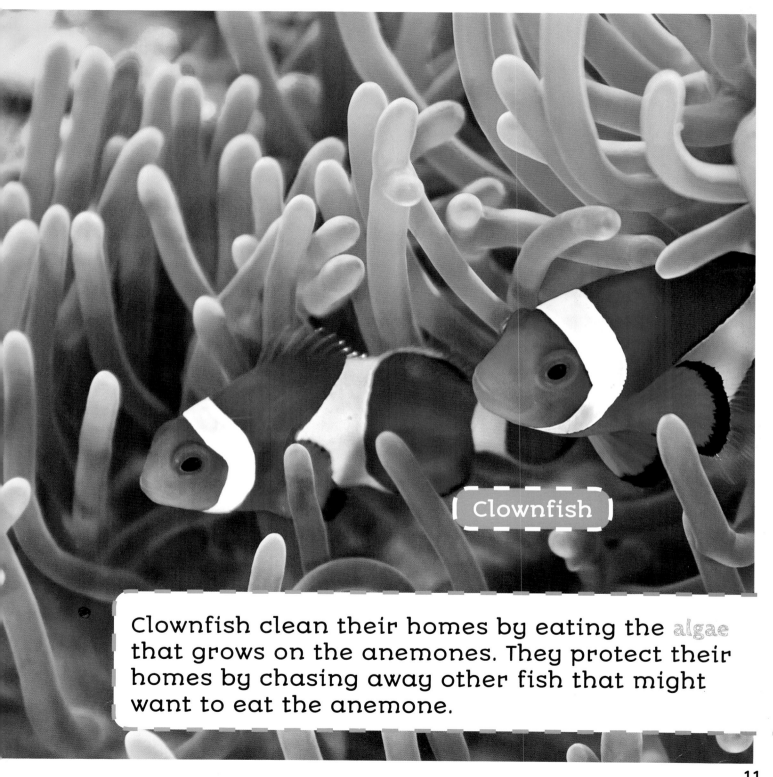

Clownfish

Clownfish clean their homes by eating the algae that grows on the anemones. They protect their homes by chasing away other fish that might want to eat the anemone.

SIXGILL SHARKS

Sixgill sharks live deep down in the ocean where light doesn't reach. They have big eyes that glow bright green in the dark to help them see.

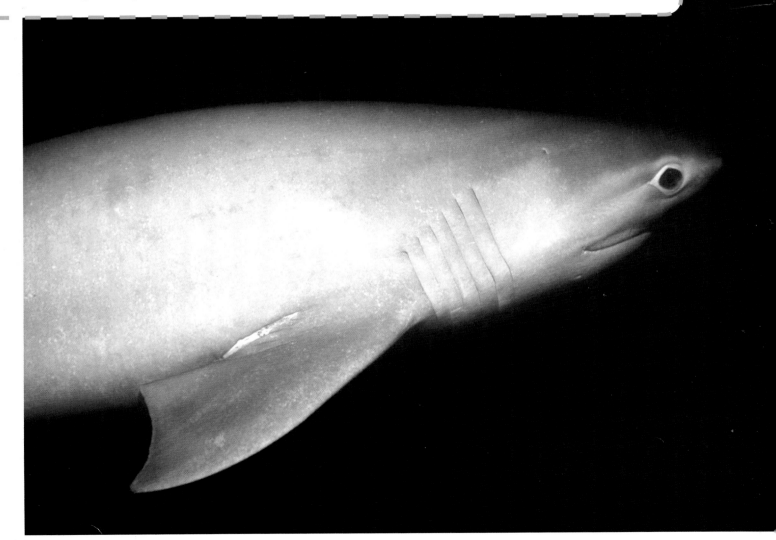

At night, these sharks will swim near the ocean's surface to hunt and scavenge. They usually eat animals like rays, crabs and other sharks.

Baby sharks, like this one, are called pups.

BLUE WHALES

Blue whales are the biggest animals on Earth. They eat tiny animals called krill. Sometimes they eat up to 40 million krill a day.

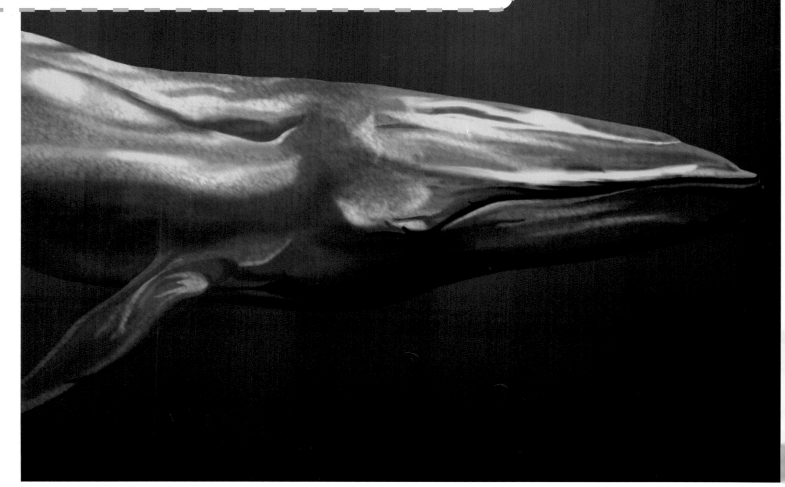

The biggest animals need the biggest homes. This is why whales live in the open ocean. They can call to other whales who are hundreds of kilometres away.

MANTIS SHRIMPS

Mantis shrimp make their homes in burrows on the ocean floor. They often stand in front of their burrow, attacking any animal that comes near it.

A mantis shrimp's punch is as fast as a bullet!

When attacking, mantis shrimps use club-like claws to smash the shells of animals like crabs and sea snails.

JELLYFISH

Jellyfish have many different homes all over the ocean. Some live deep in the dark ocean trenches and some live near the coast.

Some jellyfish can glow in the dark.

A Lion's
Mane Jellyfish

Jellyfish usually move by floating along ocean currents. To catch their prey, jellyfish drag their tentacles around them, which sting any animals they touch.

OCEANS IN
DANGER

Our ocean animals are in danger because of overfishing. Overfishing happens when people catch and eat too many fish. This can cause some animals to become endangered.

Lots of rubbish is dumped in the ocean, like plastic bags and bottles. This rubbish can harm ocean animals that try to eat it.

SCALLOPED HAMMERHEADS

Scalloped hammerheads are endangered because of overfishing. People catch these sharks for their fins to make shark fin soup.

SEA TURTLES

Endangered sea turtles often mistake pieces of plastic for jellyfish, which they like to eat. When turtles accidentally eat plastic, they can get sick and die.

You can help keep ocean animals safe by recycling your plastic rubbish.

GLOSSARY

algae	living things that are like plants, but have no roots, stems, leaves or flowers
anemone	an animal with tentacles that is usually fixed to something hard like a coral reef
burrows	a hole or tunnel dug by an animal
continents	very large areas of land that are made up of many countries, like Africa and Europe
endangered	when a species of animal is in danger of going extinct
ocean trenches	huge, narrow cuts in the ocean floor that go very deep
open ocean	an area of ocean far away from any land
prey	animals that are hunted by other animals for food
scavenge	to feed on animals that are already dead
shelter	protection from danger and harsh weather

Index